CRAFTY BAGS

for Stylish Girls

Uniquely Chic Purses, Pouches & Pocketbooks

by Elizabeth Ingrid Hauser • illustrated by Lisa Perrett

Sterling Publishing Co., Inc.

New York

Designed by Pamela Darcy of Neo9design, Inc.

The book cover featured on page 86 is from *The Return* by Daoma Winston.
Copyright © 1972 by Daoma Winston.
Used by permission of HarperCollins Publishers/Avon Books.

Velcro® is a registered trademark of Velcro Industries B.V.
Mod Podge® is a registered trademark of Plaid Enterprises, Inc.
The placemat design pictured on page 52 is the property of Jonathan Adler Enterprises LLC.
The gift wrap design pictured on page 84 is the property of Hanna Werning.
Space would not permit the inclusion of every decorative item photographed for this book, nor could all of the designers be identified.

Parental supervision is always recommended for young readers doing unfamiliar craft projects. Please pay extra attention to projects that use a hot glue gun. Although these craft projects were carefully tested, the author and publisher cannot assume responsibility for any injuries, losses, or other damages that may result from the use of the information in this book.

Library of Congress Cataloging-in-Publication Data Available

2 4 6 8 10 9 7 5 3 1

Published by Sterling Publishing Co., Inc.
387 Park Avenue South, New York, NY 10016
Copyright © 2007 by Elizabeth Ingrid Hauser
Illustrations copyright © 2007 by Lisa Perrett
Distributed in Canada by Sterling Publishing
c/o Canadian Manda Group, 165 Dufferin Street,
Toronto, Ontario, Canada M6K 3H6
Distributed in the United Kingdom by GMC Distribution Services,
Castle Place, 166 High Street, Lewes, East Sussex, England BN7 1XU
Distributed in Australia by Capricorn Link (Australia) Pty. Ltd.
P.O. Box 704, Windsor, NSW 2756, Australia

Printed in China
All rights reserved

Sterling ISBN-13: 978-1-4027-3654-4
ISBN-10: 1-4027-3654-1

For information about custom editions, special sales, premium and corporate purchases, please contact Sterling Special Sales Department at 800-805-5489 or specialsales@sterlingpub.com.

With very warm memories, I dedicate this book to my former art students in Chiang Mai, Thailand.

–E.I.H.

A very special thanks to:

• Mom, for the many glittery packages of craft supplies she sent my way

• Alex Heinke, for his help with the Yeti pin

• Carrie Chaikin, for the use of her shimmery props

• Joe Robinson, for the snappy Sass and Elizabeth photo he took, featured on page 56

• Anand Ramaswamy and Jeffrey Cranor, for their invaluable Web site expertise

• Meredith Mundy Wasinger, for being such a wonderfully thorough editor

• Karen Nelson and Pamela Darcy, for their marvelous design work

• James Levin and Jami Saunders at James Levin Studios LLC, who made the photo shoot a dream

Contents

It's All in the Bag!

A bag is not just a fashion accessory—it also keeps you fluster free. With the right tote, clutch, or purse at your side, it's easier to feel a couple of winks ahead of the game. So how do you bag your own style? Reflect on what's important to you. Are you cuckoo for animals? Does music rock your soul? Do winter sports send chills up your spine? Well, there you go! Once you know what you like, you have a sturdy platform (or shall I say runway?) upon which to build a signature style.

Who's This Book for, Anyway?

This book is for crafty gals who adore making pocketbooks of all shapes, sizes, and themes. Many of the projects spring from ready-made containers or long-forgotten bags you may have hidden at the back of your closet. So if you love breathing new life into old junk, then stay tuned!

Material Girl

Supplies are entirely in the eye of the creative beholder. I've witnessed many a seemingly fashion-savvy crafter become way too influenced by what the material or object is supposed to be for, rather than what she would like to use it for. So you want to turn that fuzzy hat upside down and add handles. Why not? Would your old scarf look better as a purse strap? Go for it! Follow your instincts and be inventive!

Crafting materials are generally not pricey, but when it comes to crafting tools, I highly recommend that you invest in good equipment. Some people think that they are saving money when they buy cheap scissors and shoddy glue. Sadly, they are in fact wasting not only money but also time and energy since they will likely become frustrated with their projects and have to start over. Don't let that happen to you!

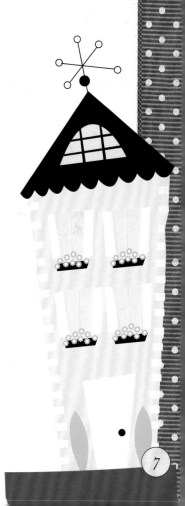

Hot Topic!

When using a hot glue gun, be careful! <u>Always</u> place a glue mat underneath to catch sticky goops and globs, and <u>always</u> unplug the tool when you are finished. If ever you are in doubt, ask for help.

The Secret Art of Glamouflage

Glamouflage is the mastery of stylish disguise. Here's the formula:

Crafty Camouflage + Glittery Glamour = GLAMOUFLAGE!!!

I never throw away a cute pocketbook just because of a little stain or two. Instead, I glamouflage it by artfully covering the blemish with decorative ribbons, a nifty brooch, or some other fabulous concoction. All you need to do is summon your creative spirit to find a clever solution.

As you work on the projects in this book—whether you are simply glamouflaging an old bag, or whipping up something completely new—it's definitely okay if your bag turns out looking different from those shown in the photos. Every handmade purse, backpack, or tote bag is a one-of-a-kind!

Glitterific!!!

As you may have guessed, sparkles are a top ingredient in many of my creative recipes. There are two principal ways to glitterize a project.

1. Trace the decorative details of your project with glue and sprinkle the glitter of your choice over the top. Shake the glittery part over a sheet of paper and save the excess. The advantage of this method is that the shimmer is super brilliant! The disadvantage is that fairy dust may trail behind you.

2. The second method is to apply glitter glue directly to the ornamental elements of your design. The advantage here is that sparkles will stay put. The disadvantage is that glitter glues are sometimes quite gloppy and the glimmer is a little more subdued.

On Using Templates . . .

Templates (AKA patterns) help bags of all kinds take on a polished, professional feel.

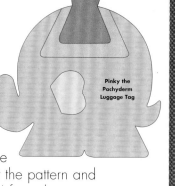

Pinky the
Pachyderm
Luggage Tag

Find your crafty templates on pages 106–111. Simply trace onto paper or photocopy the template you wish to use. If you want a different size, reduce or enlarge it. Then cut out the pattern and lay it on the flip side of your project's material. Trace the shape with a marker or pen. Lift up the pattern and there's your shape! Now cut it out and continue with your project. Since this book is all about bags (which have fronts and backs), you will often need to make two of the same form.

   Feel free to make your own patterns as well. The best way to start is with a symmetrical shape. Draw an outline on a piece of paper, then fold it in half. Choose one of the marked sides to cut along. When you are finished, unfold the pattern. Your shape should be completely the same on both sides. As for asymmetrical contours, those take more practice. I suggest sketching, cutting out, tracing, and altering (in that order) as a design exercise. In no time at all, you will be pattern-making like a pro!

Winsome Tips 'n Tricks!

When it comes to craft projects, it's crucial to have a host of tips in your creative treasury.

- Layering felt and fabric shapes is a great way to give a bag extra visual verve. These contours can be as simple or complex as you wish.

- Get a handle on it! Ribbons, scarves, strong necklaces, beaded wire, and cord, as well as craft store handles, are all ways to get a grip on your purse.

- Use bags of all kinds! Baskets, cosmetic cases, receipt bags, coin purses, and abandoned old pocketbooks are dandy as starting points for your projects.

- Proper bag closure is sometimes important. I love self-stick Velcro® dots and strips, but there are also magnets, snaps, and clasps, which can be sewn in place.

- This book only requires the most basic of sewing skills, like stitching in and out of two layers of fabric to join them. Some projects call for "tacking": First, thread your needle and tie a knot in your thread. Then position the two pieces of fabric you wish to tack together. Stitch a couple of tiny loops, joining the two pieces together. Knot the ends of your thread and snip the excess.

- When marking a pattern, I like to use a color that is just slightly darker than my material (but still of the same hue). You may also use a fabric marker, which will fade with time.

- Coating exposed fabric edges (or small decorative shapes) with a thin layer of glue is a good way to keep them from fraying.

- Drying time for projects involving craft glue or paint is usually around one or two hours. Your projects will be worth the wait!

Everyday Elegance

Is that a "boo-hoo" I hear?
The everyday bag sometimes feels
a bit underappreciated. She's
the pack mule of the bag world,
lugging daily essentials from hither
to yonder and back again.

Everyday bags need not
look humdrum, however. A
buckle here and a snazzy strap
there can make the difference
between a bag that's tiring and
one that's inspiring!

Buckle Up!

Buckle up, sweetheart! There's plenty of style ahead . . .

1. Slide the ribbon through the belt buckle so that there is plenty of material on both sides to work with.

2. Lay the ribbon and belt buckle down on your bag for placement. Then cut the ribbon so that it falls just over the top edge of your purse and just to the bottom edge.

3. Sew the buckle securely to the ribbon.

4. Fold the top section of ribbon over the top edge of the bag and sew it to the lining. If there is no lining, you may need to use glue.

5. Sew the bottom section of ribbon to the bottom edge of the bag. Again, you may need to glue it in place, especially if the leather or cloth is too stiff to stitch.

6. Allow drying time if you've used glue, throw that bag over your shoulder, and hit the road!

Sack These Supplies!

- soft leather or cloth bag (a simple one works best)
- 1 belt buckle (you can swipe one off an old belt)
- 1 long piece of thick ribbon that fits your buckle
- craft scissors
- strong needle and thread
- craft glue or hot glue gun and glue sticks (if needed)

11

No-Detention-for-You Backpack

It's a well-known fact that girls with great backpacks never get detention!

1. Round the top corners of both felt rectangles with the craft scissors to create matching arches.

2. Decorate one of the felt pieces by sewing or gluing decorative ribbons down the front, punctuated by large buttons. This will be the part of the backpack that faces out. Dashing!

3. Then cut your strong, wide ribbon into two 1-yard pieces. (These will be your straps.)

4. Time to attach your straps to the remaining piece of felt. Sew one piece of ribbon to each of the top curves of the backpack, so that both pieces loop down over the back section.

5. You might need some help from a friend to do this step. Try the straps on for size. While you're wearing the bag, ask your friend to determine the proper attachment points so that the straps rest comfortably on your shoulders and the bag doesn't sag too much. She can safety-pin each ribbon to the bag to mark the attachment points. Now slip your arms out and sew the two ribbons to the bottom, corresponding corners of the bag. (You will be sewing the ribbons not at their ends, but somewhere along their length.) Allow the rest of the ribbon to cascade down, just for decoration. Don't forget to remove the safety pins if you used them!

6. Sew the front of your bag to the back, using a simple whip stitch. To do this, insert the threaded needle into the felt from the back and pull it through to the front. Then stitch over the top of the felt edge and back through to the front. Be sure to allow ample thread to work with, and tie a knot at the end so that the thread doesn't pull right through the felt.

7. Continue with this process (making sure the stitches are evenly spaced) until your backpack is sewn together in the form of a large pocket. Knot your thread and snip the excess.

8. Add self-stick Velcro dots to the top inner edges so that your backpack can open and close properly. Smartly done. The only reason you will be kept after school is so that teachers can admire your handiwork!

Sack These Supplies!

- 2 felt rectangles (about 9" x 12" each)
- craft scissors
- several kinds of decorative ribbon
- 3 large buttons
- very strong needle
- embroidery floss or heavy-duty thread
- craft glue (if needed)
- 2 yards of wide ribbon (strong—for your straps)
- tape measure
- 2 safety pins (optional)
- several self-stick Velcro dots

What's in the bag?
A little bit of homework and an after-school snack.

Little Black Bag

This punchy pocketbook goes from day to night in a flash.

1. Using the fabric marker, transfer the gusset template from page 107 onto the back side of your polka-dotted fabric twice. Cut out both pieces. (These gussets will become the sides of your bag.)

2. Following just the *inside* of the gusset pattern (the part inside the dotted lines), cut two cardboard shapes that fit directly in the middle of the gussets but don't interfere with the fabric at the edges.

3. Glue these cardboard shapes to the back of your gussets for strength. The cardboard should now be centered on the gussets so that the fabric tabs at the edges are left loose and glue-free.

4. Fold one of your felt pieces in half so that it resembles a taco shell. The gussets will be glued in place to close the sides of your "taco" and turn it into a pouch. To do this, carefully spread a thin layer of glue on the outsides of the tabs of one of your gussets. Line up the gluey tabs with the inside edges of your "taco" so that the polka-dotted tabs are hidden inside. This is a bit tricky, and it might help to stretch some strips of tape across the gusset and the felt to help hold them in place while they dry.

5. Repeat this step with the other gusset and opposite felt edge. You should now have a little pouch!

6. For extra stability, cut a 1½" x 9" strip of cardboard and glue it to the bottom of the pouch on the inside.

7. To create your strap, glue the ends of the black lace trim or ribbon to each of the gussets on the *inside* of the bag. How strapping!

8. With the second piece of felt, measure about a third of the way down the length and cut a diagonal flap to fit over your pouch.

9. Glue or sew this flap to the inside back edge of your pouch so that the diagonal edge folds down over the front of your bag. Stick Velcro dots inside the flap and in corresponding spots on the front of the pouch so that your pocketbook can open and close.

10. For embellishment, cut one of the shapes from the scrap of patterned fabric into a handsome decorative detail. For my bag, I cut out a fan shape following the exact lines of the motif in the material.

11. Glue the fabric detail onto black felt for strength, and trim off the excess felt. Then glue or sew the adornment to the flap on your purse. Splendid!

Sack These Supplies!

- fabric marker (needs to show up on polka-dotted fabric)
- gusset template from page 107
- small piece of black and white polka-dotted fabric
- craft scissors
- 1 piece cardboard (8" x 9")
- craft glue
- needle and black thread
- 2 black felt rectangles (9" x 12" each)
- transparent tape to be used temporarily while glue dries (optional)
- ruler
- 40" of black lace trim or ribbon
- several self-stick Velcro dots
- small scrap of black and white patterned fabric. (I found a fan pattern!)

Devilish Blue Denim

Denim has a coy way of being demure yet detonating!

1. Survey your denim and determine which section would look cute as the front of the bag. For my tote, I used the front panel of a pair of overalls, but the back pockets of a pair of jeans would work dandy, too!

2. Cut out the section you've chosen and place it on another piece of denim large enough to serve as the back of your bag.

3. Trace around the front panel with the fabric marker, leaving about two inches at each side edge for fringe. Now cut out the back panel.

4. Center the front panel on top of the back panel, making sure the front panel faces out, and sew down one side, across the bottom, and up the other side (leaving the top open).

5. Now study the rest of your denim and choose a section that works as a strap. With overalls, you've lucked out since they have built-in straps that can be cut out separately and then sewn together at the top ends. With jeans, simply look for a nice long section to cut into two strips about 2 inches wide and 18 inches long. Sew these two strips together (end to end) after they're cut to make one long strap.

6. Attach the strap to your bag by either hooking the metal overall loops in place or by sewing the ends of the band of jean material to the inside seams of your bag.

7. Create fringe along the outer edges of your bag by cutting little semi-parallel snips every quarter-inch.

8. Sew or glue the fabric scraps to the front in a flower shape. For extra personality, glue the pom-pom to the middle.

9. Irresistible!!! Now accent with a devil-may-care attitude.

Sack These Supplies!

- beat-up old jeans or overalls
- craft scissors
- fabric marker
- ruler
- strong needle and thread
- several fabric scraps
- 1 pom-pom
- craft glue

What's in the bag?
Red–hot cinnamon gum to complement your Devilish Blue Denim.

Holiday Bag Bliss

'*Tis the season! Holiday bags accentuate a celebration like confetti at a carnival. What's Valentine's Day with zero romance, or Halloween without a witch or two? Easter wouldn't be so sprightly if it were shy one sassy little bunny, and the winter holidays would be ho-ho-hum in the absence of snow-frosted spruce trees. So nab some festive spirit and a bag to match!*

Love in Full Bloom

The future looks rosy when you go out on the town
with this sweet little number.

1. Arrange your fabric roses on the front of the bag and hot-glue them in place.

2. Cover the rest of the bag (front *and* back) with overlapping fabric leaves and hot-glue them in place.

3. Finally, attach your pearly necklace to the zipper pull with needle and thread or by clasping it in place (depending on the type of necklace and zipper). Tie a secure knot in your thread and snip the excess. Three cheers for Love in Full Bloom!

Sack These Supplies!

- 1 small cosmetic bag
- 8–10 large pink fabric roses
- hot glue gun and glue sticks
- several fabric leaves
- 1 short faux pearl necklace
- needle and thread
- craft scissors

The Flirty Bunny

Wink, wink—what a beguiling bunny!

1. First, enlarge the bunny body template from page 106 by 135% and trace the outline of the shape with the fabric marker onto the light pink felt.

2. Flip the template over and repeat step 1. (The reason to flip is so that the front and back of your frisky little bag will be marker-free!)

3. Bouncing along to the next step, copy the bunny hind leg template onto the remaining light pink felt. Make extra sure that the pattern is facing the proper direction so that no marker lines will be visible.

4. Next, trace the bunny ears template onto your hot pink felt so that they, too, are facing the right direction. Cut out all of your felt pieces.

5. Now place the back piece of your bunny bag down flat on your workspace (marker side up).

6. Leaving the top edge of the shape glue-free, trace the sides and bottom with a line of glue. Quickly place the front piece of the bag on top of the back piece, lining up the edges and wiping away any excess glue.

7. Allow an hour or two of drying time (sandwich the bag between layers of waxed paper under a heavy book if you wish). When the bond is secure, your bag is ready for decorating.

8. Glue the hind legs and ears in place.

9. Glitterize the inner ear for dimension and dazzle.

10. Now glue on the marabou tail, pom-pom nose, and a snip of false eyelashes for super saucy style.

11. At last, glue your ribbon handle in place and allow to dry completely. Hopping about has never been so hippity-hip!

Sack These Supplies!

- bunny template from page 106
- red or dark pink fabric marker
- light pink felt for the body
- hot pink felt for the ears
- craft scissors
- craft glue
- waxed paper and a heavy book (optional)
- iridescent pink glitter or glitter glue
- 1 small tuft of marabou
- 1 small pom-pom
- 1 sparkly, pink false eyelash
- 7–8 inches of pretty ribbon

What's in the bag?
Perhaps some colorfully wrapped candy, a handful of jelly beans, or maybe even a weensy flower bouquet!

The Haunted Dollhouse

Get ready to scare with flair!

Setting Up the Basic Haunted Dollhouse Box

1. Using your spooky-looking craft paint, paint the outside of the box the color you want your house to be. Paint the inside of the box the color you want your rooms to be.

2. Once the paint has dried, use your ruler to measure the front of the box. Using this dimension as a guideline, cut out of felt one trapezoid shape to be the front of the house, and one to be the roof. (I chose an ominous dark purple and a witchy lavender.) Glue these shapes in place.

3. Use the templates from page 111 to make a door and doorframe out of felt and fabric. You may want to make a round, oval, or square window out of the very same materials. Glue these shapes in place.

4. Turn your lace and beaded trim into shingles, window frames, spider webs, and/or gingerbread ornamentation.

5. Glue the patterned ribbon to the base your house for cobblestones, bricks, or a flower bed. Stick the eerie flowers near the door and below the window for a spooky garden.

6. Set the box upright (with the latched side on the right) so that it opens like a book.

7. Measure the width of your handle and mark this measurement on the top of the box.

8. Using the hammer and nail, pound two tiny holes where you want the handle to attach to the top of the box. (This is called *piloting*.)

9. Twist the screw eyes into the two piloted holes. (You may have to press down fairly hard as you twist the loops.) Attach the handle to the loops with the craft wire and snip off any excess with the wire clippers.

10. Now turn the page for some creepy crafty interior decorating advice. Boo!

Sack These Supplies!
(Includes the dollhouse interior and brooches, too)

- square-shaped wooden box with latch
- spooky-looking craft paint (I chose metallics)
- paintbrush
- ruler
- assortment of fabric, felt, and crafting foam pieces
- white marker or pen (to use on dark fabric)
- craft scissors
- craft glue and hot glue gun and glue sticks
- haunted dollhouse templates from pages 109–111
- various kinds of lace and beaded trim
- several inches of patterned ribbon
- a few small craft flowers
- 1 black, acrylic handbag handle
- small hammer and tiny nail
- 2 small metal screw eyes
- black craft wire
- wire clippers
- several markers to match the various fabrics
- selection of beads, buttons, sequins, and faux gems
- any discarded jewelry or thrift-store finds
- glitter or glitter glue
- tiny bit of cardboard (for the brooches)
- small fabric flower (for Winifred's hat)
- 2 large safety pins (for the brooches)

Decorating Your SPOOKtacular Pad

1. Use the dollhouse interior templates from pages 109–111 to make a grandfather clock, chandelier, skull portrait, fireplace, chaise lounge, and/or flying bats out of felt or fabric. You may want to glue some of these pieces onto the crafting foam for depth and sturdiness.

2. Transform the beads, buttons, sequins, and faux gems into doorknobs, chandelier decorations, grandfather clock parts, and portrait eyes.

3. Create chaise lounge legs, knickknacks, a chandelier base, fireplace embellishment, and extra flounce out of the discarded jewelry and/or thrift-store finds.

4. Glitterize whatever you deem necessary!

Winifred the Witch & Sooty the Black Cat Brooches

1. Use the witch doll body and black cat templates from page 110 to make little contours out of both felt and cardboard.

2. Glue the felt pieces to the cardboard pieces for strength.

3. Trace the three witch hair templates from page 110 onto alternating shades of felt.

4. Glue the bangs on top of Winifred's head.

5. Stick Winifred on top of the medium-size wig, and then stick this wig on top of the large wig. Whew! What a 'do!

6. Use the witch outfit templates from page 110 to make a hat, dress, and boots out of fabric. You will probably want to make a witch hat out of cardboard and glue it behind the fabric one so the hat doesn't flop over.

7. Complete Winifred's wardrobe with little slivers of fabric for a hat and dress sash. You may even want to outline certain parts of her outfit with the markers for more definition.

8. Dazzle up your spellbinding duo by giving them both gems for eyes and a little fabric slit of a mouth for Winifred.

9. Finally, glue the small fabric flower to Winifred's hat, just so she looks sociable.

10. Now attach the safety pins to the backs of both Sooty and Winifred: Glue little strips of felt over the stable bars of the safety pins to anchor them on to the backing material. (Hold everything firmly in place until the glue dries.) Bewitching!

Snow-Frosted Spruce Tree

Snow has a special knack for dolling up anything it touches. A plain pine one day is a spruced-up, lacy lady the next after a sprinkling of winter white!

1. On a copier, enlarge the spruce tree template from page 107 by 135%.

2. Using the marker, trace and cut out two spruce tree shapes from the felt.

3. Working from bottom to top, glue the white lace trim to one of the tree shapes in layers that resemble snowy pine boughs.

4. Glue the bottom and side edges of your lacy tree to the second felt tree, making sure that the top is left open to form a pocket.

5. Snip any excess bits of lace you don't want hanging around and then glitterize your spruce.

6. Sew the necklace in place so that it serves as a handle. O, Tannenbaum!

Sack These Supplies!

- spruce tree template from page 107
- dark green marker
- craft scissors
- green felt
- assorted pieces of white lace trim
- craft glue
- iridescent white glitter or glitter glue
- needle and green thread
- 1 sparkly necklace (not too long)

What's in the bag?

Marvelous for toting candy canes or other holiday confections!

The Captivating Clutch

The clutch is a purse with a saucy sense of humor. "Who, me? Strapped to a cumbersome handle? I'm a style icon!" She may be a little uppity, but, oh well, she has a point. The charm of the clutch really shines when the occasion calls for subdued elegance. With no handle to get in the way, the refined design acts as a canvas for your lively imagination.

The Plucky Poppy

This lone poppy is the pick of the field.

1. Take a gander at your materials and decide which felt looks best against the color of your receipt bag. Then, using the poppy template from page 109, mark and cut out your flower pieces.

2. Glitterize the edges of both flower shapes.

3. Glue the smaller poppy piece inside the bigger one.

4. Now adhere your pom-pom to the middle of the flower.

5. While everything is drying, snip your green ribbon to the desired length and glue it up one side of your bag (about an inch or so from the outside edge).

6. Finally, glue your poppy on top of its stem. Done!

Sack These Supplies!

- 1 small to medium-size receipt bag (orange or red)
- a variety of dark pink, orange, or red felt pieces (for the poppy)
- poppy template from page 109
- dark red marker
- craft scissors
- iridescent glitter or glitter glue
- craft glue
- 1 small yellow pom-pom
- a few inches of narrow green ribbon

Table for Two?

Make a reservation for you and your placemat!

1. Lay your placemat vertically, opposite of how you would lay it at the dinner table, with the good side facing down.

2. Fold the placemat so that the bottom edge comes up to cover a little over two-thirds of the rest of the placemat.

3. Sew or glue the two side edges to create a pocket.

4. Then fold the top edge down, over the pocket, creating a little flap.

5. Now add two Velcro dots to the inside flap of your clutch, and add corresponding Velcro dots where the flap folds down over the pocket.

6. For added strength and structure, measure, mark, and cut the piece of cardboard so that it fits inside your clutch.

7. Top it all off with the brooch for decoration.

8. Guess what? The two very different-looking clutches in the photo were made using exactly the same directions. The final look of your clutch depends on the materials YOU choose!

Sack These Supplies!

- 1 cloth placemat
- craft glue, hot glue gun and glue sticks, or sewing machine
- 2 self-stick Velcro dots
- ruler
- marker
- craft scissors
- 1 medium-size piece of cardboard
- 1 lovely brooch (doesn't need to be expensive)

What's in the bag?

A gift certificate for your favorite restaurant, and maybe a spare set of chopsticks!

Hoot, Hoot, Oh-So-Cute!

Style really takes flight with owls on the fashion runway.

1. Using your marker and paper, draw a simple little branch shape that is long enough to stretch across the front of the receipt bag. Cut out this shape and use it as a pattern to trace a branch onto the dark brown felt. Cut out your branch.

2. If desired, paint a wood grain pattern on your branch using craft paint and a fine-tipped paintbrush.

3. Use one of the circle stencils as a guide to make a blue felt moon.

4. For extra moonlight shimmer, glitterize the edges of your moon.

5. Now pick out six or seven pom-poms to use for the owl family. Choose a variety of sizes to represent the different family members.

6. Cut your cream, tan, and brown felt scraps into little tufted owl heads and glue them on top of your pom-poms. Don't worry too much about making the felt heads look perfect; quirky shapes will give them character!

7. Then choose which buttons would look cute as eyes, and glue those in place.

8. Now for the beaks! Snip itty-bitty felt triangles and glue them in front of the eyes.

9. Finally, cut little leaves out of your woodsy-looking fabric to embellish your branch. You may use the leaf-shaped template on page 108, if you wish, or simply cut out your own shapes.

10. Your components are all complete, so arrange and glue them in place starting with the moon, then the branch, then the owls, and lastly the leaves.

11. Allow drying time and take this clutch out on the town (or into the woods)!

Sack These Supplies!

- 1 small to medium-size receipt bag (neutral in color)
- dark brown marker
- plain paper for making a pattern
- craft scissors
- dark brown felt (for the branch)
- light brown or gold craft paint (optional)
- fine-tipped paintbrush (optional)
- circle stencils (from art or craft store)
- light blue felt (for the moon)
- iridescent blue glitter or glitter glue
- assorted cream, tan, and brown pom-poms
- tiny scraps of cream, tan, and brown felt
- craft glue or hot glue gun and glue sticks
- mismatched buttons
- woodsy-looking fabric (for the leaves)
- leaf template from page 108 (optional)

What's in the bag?

Your library card, you wise owl, you!

Tea with Marie

*Let them eat cake! (Just don't lose your head
if you spill crumbs on your regal clutch.)*

1. Enlarge the Tea with Marie templates from page 106 by 135%, and trace the large swirly shapes onto the felt.

2. Create some smaller fancy shapes of your own and mark them onto the felt as well. (You may want to experiment on paper first and then transfer the patterns.)

3. Cut out your main pieces and arrange them onto the front of your cosmetic bag. You don't have to make your bag look like the one in the picture. Half the fun of this project is coming up with new shapes!

4. If you like the way everything looks, glue the felt in place. If not, keep rearranging until you are pleased, and then glue.

5. A fetching aspect of this bag is the layering of felt. I chose to layer pink on pink, but you can choose any color palette you wish. Once your main felt pieces are dry, you may want to add smaller hearts and squiggles within them for extra visual richness and depth. What a tasty creation!

Sack These Supplies!

- 1 satiny cosmetic bag
- Tea with Marie templates from page 106
- assorted felt pieces
- marker (should match felt)
- plain paper for making a pattern (optional)
- craft scissors
- craft glue

What's in the bag?

When not being toted off to tea parties, why not use your grand new clutch for storing dress-up gloves and other finery?

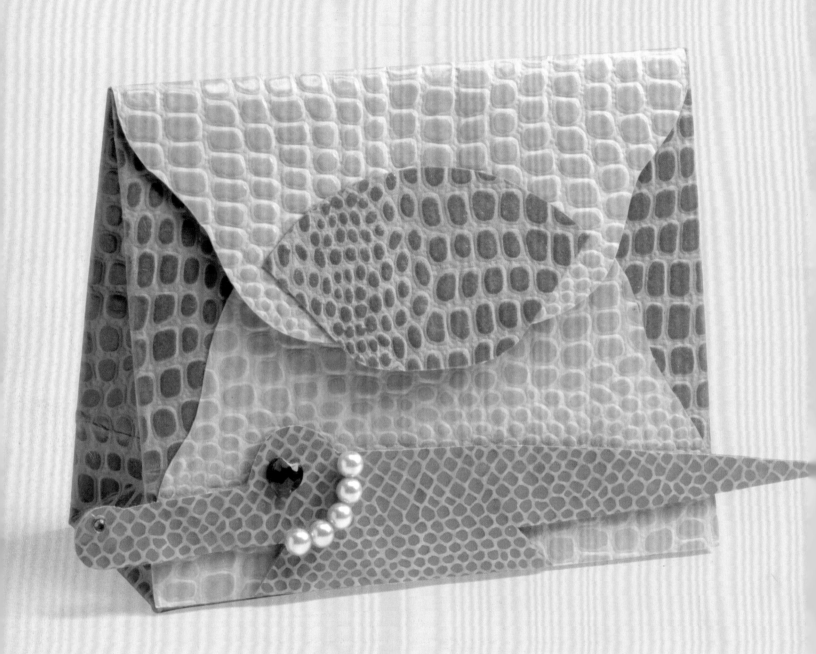

You've Got Style, Crocodile!

Most crocodile and alligator bags carry sad tales for all of the critters involved. Fortunately, no reptiles were ruined in the creation of this clever clutch!

1. Cut several inches off the top of your crocodile gift bag so that its shape is short and narrow. You might want to use the marker and ruler beforehand to make sure the line is even.

2. Measure the length and height of the front of your bag and make a plain paper pattern big enough to cover half of this area.

3. Trace the pattern twice onto your sturdy croc gift wrap and cut out the two shapes. (One will be glued to the front of the bag as decoration, and the other will serve as the flap to close your clutch.)

4. Glue the first shape to the front of your clutch, making sure that the edges (of both bag and gift wrap) line up at the bottom. This is purely for decoration.

5. Measure down about half an inch from the top edge of the second gift wrap shape and fold a long crease. You've now made a tab.

6. Glue this tab to the inner top edge of the back of your pocketbook, so that the flap folds down over the front.

7. Add self-stick Velcro dots to the underside of your flap and to the corresponding spots on the front of the bag so that it can open and close securely.

8. If desired, cut a little shape out of the leftover gift bag material and add that to your flap for extra adornment.

9. Enlarge the crocodile template from page 107 by 135%. Now trace it onto your reptilian material and also onto a piece of felt. Cut out both shapes. Glue the reptilian material to the felt for strength.

10. Gussy up your croc by gluing a heart-shaped gem for an eye, a tiny round gem for a nostril, and some pearl beads for a necklace.

11. Glue her to the front of your pocketbook. Allow drying time.

12. Now flash a toothy grin and place that cultured clutch under your arm!

Sack These Supplies!

- 1 faux crocodile/alligator gift bag (medium-size)
- craft scissors
- marker
- ruler
- plain paper to use for making a pattern
- faux crocodile/alligator gift wrap—the sturdy stuff (for the front and flap of the bag)
- craft glue
- self-stick Velcro dots
- crocodile template from page 107
- reptilian-looking material or more gift wrap (for the crocodile)
- felt (to match the material)
- 1 heart-shaped gem
- 1 tiny round gem
- 5–7 pearl beads

Gift Bag Glimmer

The ways to present a gift are endless. Is it the Birthday Girl's big night? Cupcakes to the rescue! Got a hip surprise for the friend who has everything? Maybe tiki chic is the way to go. Once you decide on the type of gift bag needed, the special details will simply pop into place.

Feathered Froufrou To Go

Take–out has never been so festive and fanciful!

1. Using the tape measure, measure the distance (from handle to handle) around one half of the top edges of your take-out container and snip two pieces of your feather trim to that length.

2. Glue both pieces of trim in place.

3. Add gems to the trim for super sparkle!

4. Now measure and cut a piece of marabou to fit your handle.

5. Using the thread, tie the length of marabou to the handle, securing it in place at every inch with small knots.

6. Wrap the gift you are giving in a fetching piece of tissue paper and place inside. How froufrou, my *petit chou chou* (that's French for *darling*)!

Sack These Supplies!

- tape measure
- 1 brightly colored take-out container (a plain white one would work, too)
- feather trim (enough to trim container)
- craft scissors
- hot glue gun and glue sticks
- 6 faux gems
- marabou (enough to cover handle)
- thread to match your marabou
- colorful tissue paper

Broken-Hearted Pocketbook

Alas, love isn't easy. If you have a friend who's weepy over a broken heart, try cheering her up with a thoughtful care bag!

1. Use the paper and marker to make a medium-size heart-shaped pattern. Transfer it onto your felt or other thick material and cut it out.

2. Again, with the paper and marker, make a lightning bolt-shaped pattern to fit the middle of the heart. Transfer it onto brightly colored felt and cut it out. If you wish, make a lightning bolt shape out of patterned fabric as well for a nice layered effect.

3. Glue these zigzag shapes on top of the heart, straight down the middle. Sniff, sniff, your heart is now broken. Set it aside for later.

4. Cut out two identical felt rectangles to form your bag. Snip the side edges so that they are jagged like your broken heart.

5. Glue these two felt pieces together at the sides and bottom, leaving an opening at the top (and therefore a pouch in the middle) and some space at the corner edges to attach the handle.

6. Glue the sides of that poor ol' broken heart to the front of the bag, leaving the top open to serve as a pocket.

7. Cut the ribbon to about 20 inches and glue it between the two felt rectangles to serve as a handle.

8. If you're feeling decorative, trim the bottom of the purse with more ribbon.

9. Now fill the bag with a few essentials guaranteed to ease a broken heart. (See "What's in the Bag?" at right.)

10. Give the Broken-Hearted Pocketbook to your most melancholy, lovesick bud. Remember, she might need a shoulder to cry on, as well.

Sack These Supplies!

- plain paper to use for making a pattern
- marker
- felt or another kind of thick material (for the heart)
- craft scissors
- small amount of brightly colored felt
- small amount of patterned fabric (optional)
- craft glue or hot glue gun and glue sticks
- 2 identical felt rectangles
- ribbon (at least 25")
- 1 lovely flowered hankie
- 1 dark chocolate bar
- 1 old key

What's in the bag?

A beautiful hankie for wiping teardrops in style, dark chocolate for melting away all those bittersweet memories, and the key to a bright, sunshiny new day.

Pampered Paw Treat Cozy

My cat Sassafras loves snacks almost as much as I do!

1. Using the tape measure, determine the height and circumference (the distance around the middle) of your cylindrical container.

2. With these measurements in mind, draw a rectangle using the pencil and ruler on the back side of your animal print wrapping paper. (I chose zebra print.) Cut it out and try it on your cylinder. Trim carefully until you have the perfect fit.

3. Seal the paper rectangle around your container with Mod Podge craft adhesive (read the directions on the package). It's very important to work creases out as you go along!

4. While the container is drying, hot glue a short snip of the marabou to the ponytail band.

5. Then draw two ears and a little critter mask onto your thick animal print paper or cardboard. My shapes are very catlike, but you can choose any creature for inspiration.

6. Now pick out the circle stencil that best fits the container lid and mark a circle of this size on the same thick animal print paper.

7. Cut out all of these shapes and seal them with Mod Podge so that they are waterproof.

8. Allow drying time and then hot-glue the circle to the lid.

9. Next comes the fun part! Arrange and glue the ears and animal mask to the front of your container. Then add the oval or marquis-shaped gems for the eyes and the heart gem nose.

10. Slip the marabou band around the bottom of your container.

11. Very glamorous! Now hot-glue the pipe cleaner up the back of the container and curlicue it around to make a tail handle.

12. You may want to glue a little patch of sealed animal print paper over the base of your tail to make sure it is extra secure.

13. Fill up the dazzling treat cozy with dry cat or dog snacks and give it to your pet-crazy friend!

Sack These Supplies!

- 1 clean cylindrical pet treat container
- tape measure
- pencil
- ruler
- animal print wrapping paper (enough to wrap around the container)
- craft scissors
- Mod Podge® craft adhesive (it even comes in a sparkly version!)
- hot glue gun and glue sticks
- ponytail band
- marabou trim (to cover the ponytail band)
- animal print cardboard or thick craft paper (for the ears, mask, and lid)
- circle stencils (from art or craft store)
- 2 oval or marquis-shaped gems
- 1 tiny heart-shaped gem
- 1 fuzzy pipe cleaner
- dry cat or dog snacks

Sugarbomb Birthday Wishes!

Happy birthday to you! Your style is on cue.
You're cute as a cupcake and as sweet as one, too!

1. Enlarge the cupcake template from page 106 by 135% and trace the whole outline of the cupcake onto one piece of paper with the pencil. Cut it out. This will be the back of your bag.

2. Pick which paper you wish to use for the frosting, the cherry, and the baking cup. Use the three different segments of the template to copy these pieces individually onto the paper you have chosen for each.

3. Cut out your cupcake shapes and glue the frosting to the baking cup, making sure the front shapes will line up with the contour of the back piece when you are ready to join them.

4. Top the frosting with the cherry.

5. Now, just at the sides and bottom of the baking cup, glue the front of the bag to the back, leaving an opening at the top and a pouch in the middle.

6. Decorate your cupcake with colorful sequins.

7. Glue your ribbon to the bag (between the front and the back) as a little cherry stem handle.

8. Scrumptious! Now allow drying time and slip a tiny card inside for the birthday girl. (See "What's in the bag?" at right.)

Sack These Supplies!

- cupcake template from page 106
- a variety of yummy-looking paper
- pencil
- craft scissors
- craft glue
- colorful sequins
- 5–6 inches of narrow ribbon
- gift card

What's in the bag?

The Sugarbomb is also très adorable for holding a little gift card for the recipient's favorite store!

Cheeky Tiki Tote

Nothing says "luau" like a little tiki chic!

1. Using your ruler and marker, draw a little 5" x 6" rectangle (or slightly larger) on your plain paper. Cut out this shape and fold it in half lengthwise.

2. Now cut the edges opposite the fold at a slight angle. Open up the shape and you have an isosceles trapezoid!

3. Use this trapezoid pattern to mark two tiki shapes on the woven placemat. Cut out both shapes.

4. Ah . . . the fun part! Cut cute tiki-face features out of your placemat scraps or felt scraps and make a pretty tropical flower out of shiny fabric, felt, or both. (You may want to make paper patterns first.)

5. Glue these shapes in place on your tiki face and add beads, a tiny pom-pom, or glitter for decoration.

6. While everything is drying, cut little flower shapes out of the felt and the netting. String them together on the long piece of craft wire alternating them between the beads and the beadable pom-poms to make a lei handle. If you wish to include any glitterized pom-poms, add the sparkly stuff beforehand.

7. When you have beaded about ten inches, stop and clip your flowery garland, allowing plenty of extra wire on both ends for attaching your handle. "Lei" it aside for later!

8. Now glue the two tiki trapezoid shapes together at the sides and bottom, leaving an opening at the top and space to attach your handle. If your shapes aren't taking to the craft glue, use hot glue instead.

9. You're almost there! Attach the handle to the tote by poking the wire ends through the top side edges of the woven tote and twisting them back around the stem of the lei securely. Clip the excess wire with the wire clippers.

10. Dance a little hula in celebration of a job well done!

Sack These Supplies!

- marker
- ruler
- plain paper to use for making a pattern
- craft scissors
- 1 pliable woven placemat
- assorted scraps of woven placemats
- assorted felt scraps
- shiny fabric (optional)
- craft glue or hot glue gun and glue sticks
- assorted beads
- tiny pom-pom (optional)
- glitter or glitter glue (optional)
- netting
- 1 long piece of craft wire (for the handle)
- assorted beadable pom-poms
- wire clippers

What's in the bag?

This tote is great for giving tropical umbrellas and fancy straws to the luau hostess at her pool party. If you wish to make a lei for her (or for yourself), just follow the handle instructions in step 6 and keep on going!

Techy Totes & Posh Portfolios

There's a cryptic aura that surrounds techy totes and posh portfolios. What IS she hiding in there? Could it be a haunted house detector, or an alien tracking device? Maybe it's a mysterious mermaid's undersea treasure map leading to vast sums of glistening sunken gold? Okay, okay, so it's just a cell phone and your latest art project . . . but by all means, dear, keep them guessing!

Chitterly Chatterbag

*This cell phone tote is a gas as long as
you don't turn into a total windbag!*

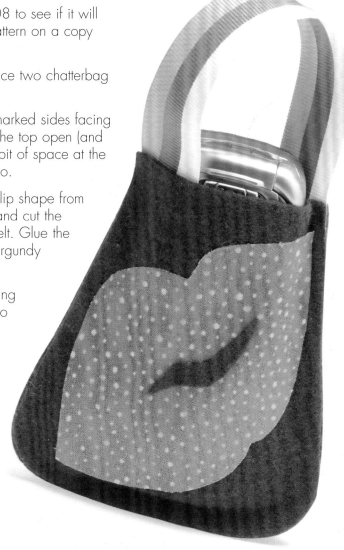

1. Measure the chatterbag template from page 108 to see if it will fit your cell phone. If it does not, enlarge the pattern on a copy machine for the perfect fit.

2. Once you have the properly sized template, trace two chatterbag shapes onto your burgundy felt.

3. Cut these shapes out and glue them together, marked sides facing inward, around the sides and bottom, leaving the top open (and therefore a pouch in the middle). Also leave a bit of space at the top two corner edges where your handle will go.

4. While the bag is drying, mark and cut out the lip shape from the template onto your pink fabric. Then mark and cut the little inner pucker shape out of your burgundy felt. Glue the fabric lips to the front of your bag. Glue the burgundy felt pucker in the middle of the lips.

5. Glue the ribbon in place as a handle. Depending on its width, you may need to glue the ribbon to just one side of the felt edge (to leave room for your cell phone).

6. Allow drying time while chatting with your best bud!

Sack These Supplies!

- chatterbag template from page 108
- dark brown marker
- burgundy felt (for the bag)
- craft scissors
- craft glue
- pink patterned fabric (for the lips)
- 7–8 inches pink ribbon

Songbird Music Cozy

Tweet! Tweet! Keep your little high-tech music maker all safe and snuggly by stowing it!

1. Measure the birdcage template from page 108 to see if it will fit your little music player. If it does not, reduce or enlarge the pattern on a copy machine to fit.

2. Now use this template to mark and cut two cage outlines out of the felt and one cage outline out of the piece of striped fabric.

3. Glue the fabric birdcage directly on top of one of the felt shapes. This will be the decorative front side.

4. Glue these shapes to the back felt shape, just around the sides and bottom, leaving an opening at the top and a pouch in the middle.

5. Then, using the songbird template from page 108, make a fowl little friend out of a combination of the patterned fabric and the felt scraps. You can look at the photo to get ideas or make up your own. Also, for the birdie body, you may want to layer fabric on top of felt for sturdiness.

6. Do the same with the branch and leaf pieces, using the template from page 108.

7. Glue the branch and leaves to the base of the cage and then stick the songbird shapes on top of them.

8. Get a bird's-eye view by adding an oval gem for a cute little peeper.

9. Almost there! Cut a loop from the gold cord and tack it with the needle and thread to the top edge of the cage.

10. Allow ample drying time and take your music maker out for a stroll in the park!

Sack These Supplies!

- music cozy template from page 108
- fabric marker
- craft scissors
- 2 pieces of felt (about 5" x 6")
- striped fabric (about 5" x 6")
- craft glue or hot glue gun and glue sticks
- patterned fabric (blue shown here—for the bird)
- assorted scraps of felt in contrasting colors (blue, yellow, and brown shown here)
- 1 small scrap of green fabric
- 1 pretty oval-shaped gem
- gold cord (for the loop)
- strong needle and thread

Virtuoso Placemat Portfolio

Here's a tote for the talented-and-tasteful-on-the-go.

1. Glue the two placemats together at the sides and bottom (good sides facing out) to form a pocket. Allow drying time.

2. Attach the bag handles by looping the ribbon around the attachment points, snipping the excess ribbon, and tacking the ends with the needle and thread to the top center edges of your portfolio.

3. Using the ruler and marker, measure, mark, and cut the piece of cardboard to be slightly smaller than your portfolio. Slip it inside to provide structure for your smart new case. The cardboard will also act as a divider, so that you can keep several works of art flat and in pristine condition.

Sack These Supplies!

- 2 large, matching cloth placemats
- craft glue or hot glue gun and glue sticks
- 1 set of sew-on bag handles
- ribbon to match handles (narrow enough to slip through your handles' attachment loops)
- craft scissors
- strong needle and thread (thread color should match handles)
- ruler
- marker
- 1 large piece of cardboard

What's in the bag?

Look out, Louvre! Masterpieces galore are on their way!

53

Agent Scarlett's Attaché Case

*I simply adore scare tactics! Flaunt your venomous vogue
by arriving to class with this sinister beauty.*

1. Study your briefcase or portfolio and decide where you want the center of the spiderweb to be.

2. Using your ruler, measure and cut one piece of the thin, white ribbon so that it starts at the center of what will be your web and ends just beyond the edge of the bag.

3. Glue this piece of ribbon in place and repeat the process in rotation, forming triangular wedges like slices of pie.

4. Then cut and glue small pieces of the thin, white ribbon around the center point of the web to form the inner structure.

5. Repeat this process, forming a second shape around the first one.

6. Now cover up the ends of the web strands by trimming the outer edges of your attaché case with the red and black polka-dotted ribbon. (It's good to start and finish gluing at the bottom of the case so that the ends are hidden.)

7. While the glue is drying, mark and cut out your spider pieces, using the spider template from page 109. Make sure to use the red felt for the main part of the body and legs. Use the white pen when marking your black felt (so that you can see the line).

8. Next, glue your spider gal layers together (red-black-red).

9. Now, sparkle up your web by dabbing glue at intersecting pieces of white ribbon and then sprinkling glitter on those spots.

10. Position Agent Scarlett on her shimmery web and glue her in place!

Sack These Supplies!

- 1 small, black briefcase or portfolio
- ruler
- 1–2 yards of narrow white ribbon
- craft scissors
- craft glue
- 1–2 yards of red and black polka-dotted ribbon
- dark red marker
- spider template from page 109
- 1 piece of red felt (for the spider)
- white pen or fabric marker
- 1 small piece of black felt
- iridescent white glitter or glitter glue

What's in the bag?

*A magnifying glass, invisible ink,
top-secret correspondence,
and other crucial spy gear!*

Snappy Picture Pouch

Say "cheese" and try not to blink!

1. Choose a patterned fabric that goes well with the cosmetic bag you are using. Cut out a cute shape (a duckie for me!)

2. Glue this shape onto a piece of matching felt and trim around the edges.

3. Then, using the circle stencil, mark the size frame you would like for your picture onto a piece of pretty colored felt.

4. Inside this circle, mark the size you would like for your photo window.

5. Cut out both the outer circle and inner circle so that you now have a donut shape.

6. Now trace a circle that is a little bit bigger than your photo window onto the clear vinyl. Cut out the piece.

7. Carefully, carefully trace the vinyl circle's outer edge with glue and stick it to the back side of your donut-shaped felt frame so that it covers the photo window.

8. If you have room, mark and cut out a couple of extra felt circles to use as decoration.

9. For extra glam, tack the pom-pom onto the zipper pull using the needle and thread.

10. Lay your cosmetic bag down and decide how you want the frame and decorative details to adorn it.

11. Glue the pieces in place. Take care to adhere *only* the bottom and sides of the frame so that there is a pocket left for your photograph at the top.

12. Trim the photo to fit your picture frame and slide it into place. Picture perfect!

Sack These Supplies!

- 1 small, padded cosmetic bag
- patterned fabric (I found some with rubber duckies!)
- craft scissors
- craft glue
- assorted felt pieces
- circle stencil (from art or craft store)
- marker
- 1 snappy photo (you may want to use a copy)
- clear vinyl (to cover the photo)
- pom-pom (optional)
- needle and thread (optional)

What's in the bag?

A small, lightweight camera will fit nicely in this pouch.

A Bag 4 All Seasons

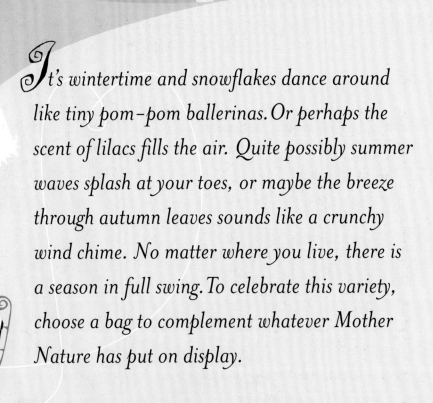

It's wintertime and snowflakes dance around like tiny pom-pom ballerinas. Or perhaps the scent of lilacs fills the air. Quite possibly summer waves splash at your toes, or maybe the breeze through autumn leaves sounds like a crunchy wind chime. No matter where you live, there is a season in full swing. To celebrate this variety, choose a bag to complement whatever Mother Nature has put on display.

Warm 'n Toasty Hat Bag

Some might get hotheaded when they see how CAP-tivating your new bag is!

1. Turn that old hat upside down and decide where you want the handles to be on your new purse.

2. Sew the handles in place at each corner.

3. Stick the Velcro dots to the top, middle, inside edges of your bag.

4. Now that your bag has closure, add the cute flower pin or brooch to the outside for decoration. Wow! Hats off to you!

Sack These Supplies!

- 1 brightly colored old hat
- 1 set of handbag handles
- needle and strong thread (should match color of handles)
- several self-stick Velcro dots
- 1 cute flower pin or brooch

Muff Purse

1. Lay your polar fleece flat. Down each of the two long sides, mark a line that is about two inches from the edge.

2. Starting from the top, snip careful parallel cuts into the fleece to create fringes that are each half an inch wide.

3. When both sides are cut into fringes, fold the polar fleece in half, widthwise, so that the fringies match up. The marked edges should face inward, and the fold should be on the bottom.

4. Starting at the top (opposite the fold), tie the two corresponding pieces of fringe into a knot on one side. Continue down the edge until all of the fringey snips are tied together. If you have one lone fringe left over (which happens sometimes), just push it through to the inside. Repeat this process with the other side. You should now have a long pouch.

5. Cut the self-stick Velcro strip so that it's not quite as wide as the pouch opening. Fasten the "loop" side of the Velcro to one of the inner edges. Attach the "hook" side of the Velcro to the opposite edge so the two match up.

6. Measure another strip of Velcro (same length as before) and stick the "loop" side along the bottom, folded edge.

7. Now fold the top of the pouch over, toward the bottom, so that it covers the top third of the bag.

8. Stick the "hook" strip of Velcro to the top folded edge of this section. Fold the bag in half so that the two Velcro strips stick together. Grrr! You now have a little muff purse.

Glamourpuff Yeti Muff

Practically perfect: this muff stores your stuff <u>and</u> keeps your hands warm!

Yeti Pin

1. Time to get Yeti-glam creative! First glue your large pom-poms together to form the body.

2. Then add your small pom-poms for the arms and legs.

3. Fuzz it up by gluing little snips of white faux fur around the head and the arms.

4. Now decorate the face by cutting the felt scraps into tiny decorative shapes. I used pink felt for a mouth, white for the tufts and teeth, tan for the claws, and brown for the eyes.

5. To make your Yeti claws even more fierce, try outlining the contour in brown marker.

6. For glitzy necklace glam, glue the two snips of gold cord and the heart-shaped gem to her front.

7. Sassy footwear can be made by cutting the fancy fabric scraps into boots and gluing them onto pink felt for strength. You can really deck them out by outlining the shape with pink marker and adding extra bits of fabric for laces!

8. Make sure all the Yeti pieces are secured and dry. Then glue her to a small piece of white felt (trimmed to hide behind her contour) for strength.

9. Attach a large safety pin to her back by gluing a small strip of felt over the stable bar of the pin. Hold on tight until the glue dries.

10. Growlingly gorgeous! When everything is dry, pin her to your muff purse and prepare for a long winter expedition!

Muff Purse History

Muff purses were very popular in the late 1800s and early 1900s. They were often made of luxurious materials such as fur, silk, or velvet.

Sack These Supplies!
For the Muff Purse

- 1 piece of polar fleece 12" x 36"
- marker (in a color that blends with your fleece fabric)
- ruler
- craft scissors
- 2 9" strips of self-stick Velcro

For the Yeti Pin

- craft glue or hot glue gun and glue sticks
- 2 large white or cream pom-poms
- 4 small white or cream pom-poms
- fuzzy, white, faux fur material or trim (for the fur)
- craft scissors
- assorted scraps of pink, white, tan, and brown felt
- brown marker
- 2 snips of gold cord (like the kind for wrapping gifts)
- 1 heart-shaped gem
- scraps of fancy fabric (I found snakeskin print)
- dark pink marker
- 1 large safety pin

The Thrifty Mermaid's Seashell Satchel

Spend a sunny day at the beach cruising waves and collecting seashells!

1. Cut your salvaged blue and/or green net and old swimsuit material into long, wavy, seaweed-like shapes.

2. Glue these shapes all the way around the top edge of your net bag so that they cascade down in a flowing manner.

3. Your satchel is now shipshape! To make a little matching beach clutch, decorate your mesh receipt bag with the same material that you used for your satchel and add the plastic seashell or starfish for oceanic embellishment.

4. No beach in your future? Don't sweat it! This satchel stows all kinds of collections: pretty rocks, rubber duckies—you name it!

Sack These Supplies!

- 1 small mesh laundry bag (the kind for washing delicates)
- assorted scraps of blue and/or green net material salvaged from an old laundry bag
- assorted scraps of blue and/or green material from old swimsuits
- craft scissors
- hot glue gun and glue sticks
- 1 plastic mesh receipt bag (optional)
- 1 plastic seashell or starfish (optional)

What's in the bag?

Although built for collecting shells, the Thrifty Mermaid's Seashell Satchel is dandy for any gets-super-sandy beach gear such as flip-flops and Frisbees. The beach clutch is wonderful for soda-pop change or sunglasses.

Bamboozled!

Have you been hoodwinked by the stylish sway of bamboo?
Just for fun, try an autumn–inspired color palette!

1. Decide which placemats you would like to use for the stalks of your plants. Mark and cut out three tall bamboo-like shapes. For extra artful oomph, cut segmented pieces to place inside the stalks.

2. Then mark and cut the bamboo leaves. If any edges (stalk or leaf) are fraying, now is the time to coat them with glue.

3. Determine the placement of the stalks on the bag and glue them in place. Do the same with the leaves.

4. Allow one to two hours of drying time . . . and then *fall* in love with your handiwork.

Sack These Supplies!

- 1 basket-style bag
- assorted woven and cloth placemats
- marker (slightly darker than color of placemats)
- craft scissors
- craft glue or hot glue gun and glue sticks

What's in the bag?

This bag is keen for collecting brightly colored leaves. When you get them home, press them under a heavy book between two sheets of waxed paper.

Tisket Tasket Snack Basket

A–picnicking you go! Just be wary of any fanged critters you may meet along the way. . . .

1. Decide which ribbon you would like for your handle and cut it to about 9 to 12 inches. (The length of ribbon needed will depend on the size of your basket.)

2. Examine your basket and determine which sides are the best ones for gluing your handle onto. Be careful! You don't want your handle placement to interfere with the opening and closing of your basket lid (if it has one). I glued mine directly to the lid to avoid any problems.

3. Glue that handle securely in place!

4. Now glue more ribbon around the edges of your basket for decoration.

5. Don't go out to lunch just yet! Embellish the front of your creation by gluing the two leaves in place and then the decorative butterfly. Make that winged bug sparkle by adding a marquis-shaped gem to the middle.

6. Tuck a cute little checkered napkin in your basket, and pack some tasty snacks for you and a friend.

7. Springtime picnic, anyone?

Sack These Supplies!

- 1 small basket (open or with a lid that clasps shut)
- assorted long pieces of plaid, gingham, and polka-dotted ribbon
- craft scissors
- craft glue or hot glue gun and glue sticks
- 2 decorative craft leaves
- 1 decorative craft butterfly
- 1 marquis-shaped gem
- 1 checkered fabric napkin
- snacks

What's in the bag?

A dainty snack for a dainty basket.

The Pint-Sized Punch of Mini Bags

What's itsy-bitsy, teeny-weeny, and even smaller than a polka-dot bikini? Why, it's a mini bag, of course! Although petite, she's quite a styling, beguiling force to contend with.

Queen of Hearts Lip Gloss Tote

Take it from the Queen of Hearts: lips without gloss are like cake without icing.

1. Fold the ribbon in half to make a loop shape. Glue this loop to the inner left edge of your lip gloss tote as a handle.

2. If your tote needs some rickrack embellishment across the top (mine did!), now is the time to measure, snip, and glue it in place.

3. Then cut your felt into two little hearts (you may want to make a paper pattern first) and glitterize the edges.

4. Glue one heart upright in the top left corner and the other heart upside down in the bottom right corner.

5. Stick or glue the decorative red "Q" in middle of the upright heart.

6. Now place your flower at the end of the loop handle and glue it securely.

7. Allow drying time and pop in some shimmery gloss!

Sack These Supplies!

- 1 red lip gloss tote
- 1 ribbon (13"–14")
- rickrack (to coordinate with ribbon)
- craft scissors
- craft glue or glue gun and glue sticks
- tiny bit of black felt
- paper to make a pattern (optional)
- glitter or glitter glue
- small, red letter "Q" (check the scrapbooking aisle of a craft store)
- 1 black or red craft flower

Wry Baby Wristlet

Oh, baby! Hard to guess that such a cutie started out as just a mesh bag.

1. Unspool about two feet of the yarn and thread your needle.

2. Leaving a five- or six-inch tail of yarn dangling down, start weaving at the top of your bag (opposite the end with the zipper pull). Continue to weave the yarn in and out of one line of holes all the way across the front of your bag. You will need to open the purse in order to do this. Be careful not to weave the two sides together!

3. When you get to the end, turn the bag over and weave across the other side.

4. When you come to the edge again, snip your yarn to match the length of the first tail. Now tie the two pieces of yarn together in a tidy little knot. The dangling yarn will become a fringe.

5. Repeat these steps with each row of holes until they are all filled.

6. Secure the bracelet to the zipper pull by winding yarn around the bracelet and then through the metal loops of the pull. Tie the yarn ends in a knot. You may want to do this several times to be sure the bracelet is tied on securely. Presto! Your wristlet is ready to roam!

Sack These Supplies!

- 1 small mesh receipt bag
- yarn (enough to cover the bag)
- 1 large crafting needle (must be big enough to thread yarn)
- craft scissors
- 1 bracelet

What's in the bag?
Movie tickets for you and a favorite gal pal!

Life-in-the-Fast-Lane Coin Purse

*Ladies, start your engines and rev up those racing stripes,
'cause this is one speedy little number!*

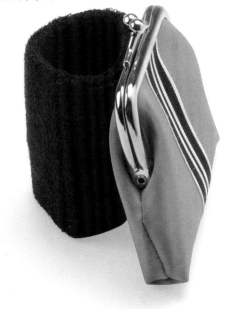

1. Glue the wristband upright to the back of your coin purse. Make sure that it is very well secured.

2. Cut your racing stripe of a ribbon to the desired length and glue it up the middle of the front of your coin purse.

3. Switch gears and try your purse on for size.

4. Glide on into the winner's circle wearing your nimble new creation on your wrist, upper arm, or even on your ankle while you're on the go!

What's in the bag?
*A purse this portable is dandy
for keys, change, and ID.*

Sack These Supplies!

- 1 inexpensive, lightweight coin purse
- 1 stretchy wristband
- hot glue gun and glue sticks
- 1 short scrap of striped ribbon
- craft scissors

Beaded Reverie Compact

Do you dream of beads and bangles? Well, here's your bag!

1. Pick the circle stencil that best represents the size of your compact.

2. Draw this circle onto your fabric and cut it out.

3. Now do something a little odd and cut diagonally across the top of your circle, about one-third of the way down. The bigger piece will become the pocket. (Be sure to save the smaller scrap, too.)

4. If you would like to glaze the edge of your pocket with glue so that the ends don't fray, now is the time.

5. Leaving the straight edge glue-free, coat the rounded perimeter of the pocket with glue and stick it in place on the front of your compact. Now you have a pocket!

6. Using your bead wire for a stem, thread the small beads to make a handle that fits your creation. The handle can be attached by poking holes in the compact fabric and looping the ends of the wire around a couple of times, or by having the ends of the wire extend under the compact hinge, meeting and joining in the middle.

7. Using the same technique as in step 6, thread more small beads onto a new length of wire to make two loop shapes. Then thread the excess wire through the large flower bead, twist, and clip the excess.

8. Cut two or three leafy shapes out of the leftover scrap of fabric and glue them to your blossoming flower. You may use the leaf-shaped template from page 108, or simply cut out your own leaf shapes.

9. Glue the beaded floral arrangement to the compact.

10. Allow drying time and tote along on your next trip to the powder room.

Sack These Supplies!

- 1 fabric compact with a built-in mirror (makeup companies often give these away!)
- circle stencils (from art or craft store)
- pretty fabric that matches your compact
- 1 marker (slightly darker than your fabric)
- craft scissors
- craft glue
- strong bead wire
- an assortment of small matching beads
- wire clippers
- 1 large flower bead
- leaf template from page 108 (optional)

What's in the bag?

There's a handy, built-in mirror on the inside, and the pocket on the outside holds cash and a few folded tissues. Perfect for powder room emergencies!

Strawberry Sunshine

Strawberries are so bloomin' sweet, why shouldn't they have their own bag?!

1. Place your strawberry basket on the green felt and trace around the base.

2. Cut out this piece and lay it flat in the bottom of the basket as a liner. Save the scraps.

3. Decide which ribbon you would like to serve as your handle and cut it to desired length (about seven inches).

4. Glue the ribbon in place so that it reaches across the top of your basket.

5. Trim your basket with ribbon and ruffles. You can even weave some pieces in and out of the plastic ribbing of the basket, gluing the ends of the ribbon together in back.

6. Using the templates from page 108, mark your strawberry pieces on the felt (stem on green, large berry shape on light pink, small berry shape on dark pink) and cut them out.

7. Now use the template from page 108 to mark your leaf on the patterned green fabric and cut that out.

8. Glue all of your strawberry pieces together and add those weensy pom-poms to the top for super sweetness.

9. Stick this delectable pink and green creation onto the front of your basket. Berry cute!

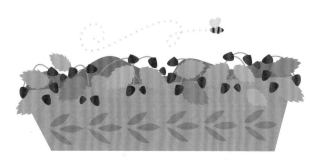

What's in the bag?

Believe it or not, there are things besides strawberries that look cute stowed in this basket . . . like medium-to-large pom-poms and ribbon (in pink, of course).

Curiously Cool

Some bags love to stand out in a crowd. They're in a lofty league of their own, making up the rules as they go along. Such is the case with the curiously cool pocketbook. She's all about off-beat outlandishness and adores showing off. Just be careful not to wear garments that compete with her spunky spirit. More often than not, this bag IS the outfit!

Ruffled Oatmeal

Wow! What a frilly makeover!

1. Using your ruler and craft scissors, snip a 12-inch piece of ribbon for your handle. Glue each end to the outside of your oatmeal container, about two inches down from the top. This part of the handle will be covered by the other ribbons that you'll be gluing around the container. The overlapping ribbons will give the handle extra strength, too.

2. Then measure, cut, and glue a pretty piece of trim or ribbon around the circumference of your container, just below the top edge.

3. Repeat this step, working your way down and around, until the container is completely trimmed.

4. Then pick the circle stencil that fits your lid and mark one circle on both your fabric and your felt. Cut them out and glue the fabric circle to the felt one. Glue this double-ply circle into the center of your lid.

5. Now trim the lid rim with rickrack, if desired. This is also the time to add decorative roses or the tassel if you wish. (Poke a hole in the bottom, slip the tassel through, and tape it securely from the inside.) Fill with girly gear!

Sack These Supplies!

- 1 empty oatmeal container
- ruler
- craft scissors
- glue gun and glue sticks
- assorted pieces of ribbon, ruffled lace, fringe, and/or pom-pom trim (long enough to wrap around the container)
- circle stencils (from art or craft store)
- marker
- 1 small piece of fabric
- 1 small piece of felt (in a color that will match the fabric)
- rickrack (optional—for the lid)
- 10 small decorative roses (optional)
- 1 medium-size tassel (optional)
- strong tape (optional)

The Lady Pirate

Anne Bonny. Mary Read. Do these names ring a brutish bell?
Lady pirates really did sail the seven seas! So let out your
fiercest "YAR!" while showing off your barbaric bon ton.

1. Cut the red fishnet tights into an assortment of shredded-looking pieces.

2. Hot-glue the larger pieces to your black bag in a helter-skelterish fashion, with some snippets stretching across the surface and others hanging down loosely.

3. Then pinch the smaller pieces and hot-glue them so that they flare out a little, adding shape and dimension.

4. Using the pirate templates from page 111, trace the skull and crossbones onto your white felt.

5. Then trace the two crossbones again, this time onto your red and white fabric.

6. Cut out all of these pirate-worthy pieces.

7. Now, using your craft glue, adhere the red and white fabric crossbones to the felt ones (this is for added strength).

8. Sparkles ahoy! Glitterize all three shapes.

9. Glue crossbone to crossbone to form an X.

10. Then glue your skull on top of the menacing crossbones.

11. Add the small heart-shaped gems as eyes and the tiny one as a nose.

12. Draw teeth and eyebrows with the black marker.

13. Fierce work, matey. Keep it up! Now hot-glue the skull and crossbones to your bag.

14. Beware, ye land lubbers! The Lady Pirate is now ready to plunder!

Sack These Supplies!

- 1 black receipt bag
- 1 pair red fishnet tights
- craft scissors
- hot glue gun and glue sticks
- pirate templates from page 111
- white felt (for skull and crossbones)
- red and white fabric (for crossbones)
- craft glue
- iridescent glitter or glitter glue
- 2 small red heart-shaped gems
- 1 tiny red heart-shaped gem
- fine-point permanent black marker

What's in the bag?

The Lady Pirate bag is for booty that baffles.
No one but YOU should know what's inside!

Prince Not-So-Charming

Better watch out, Sir Froggy–poo. Princess is at the wheel, and if your manners have been a little murky, she may decide to teach you a lesson!

1. Enlarge the frog and crown templates from page 108 by 135%. Trace the frog shape onto both your menacing fabric and your matching felt. Cut out both shapes.

2. Glue the fabric frog to the felt one (for strength) and glue on the two red heart-shaped gems for fiendish eyes.

3. Using the enlarged crown template, trace and cut out a little crown from the yellow felt and glitterize the edges.

4. Lay your file folder flat and arrange the black lace trim and rickrack in a semi-diagonal line across the front to look like a tire track (lace in the middle, rickrack on either edge). Cut the lace and rickrack to proper length and hot-glue them in place.

5. Then add the startled frog and his toppled-off crown to the composition. (Keep in mind you're not running him over—just scaring him into better behavior!)

6. Now hot-glue Prince-Not-So-Charming and his crown securely onto the bag.

7. If you need more room inside the bag for your gear, carefully cut the inner plastic dividers from your file folder so that there is space in the middle. Be sure to leave the expanding edges intact since they hold the bag together.

8. If one of your ex-princes is nearby, show him the purse he has inspired!

Sack These Supplies!

- frog and crown templates from page 108
- pretty yet slightly menacing fabric (for the frog)
- felt to match menacing fabric (for the frog)
- marker
- craft scissors
- craft glue or hot glue and glue sticks
- 2 red heart-shaped gems
- small scrap of yellow felt
- iridescent glitter or glitter glue
- expanding file folder (with built-in handle)
- black lace trim (2 inches wide—for the tire track)
- black rickrack (for the tire track)

What's in the bag?
Anything but love letters, that's for sure!

Cereal Style

A box this versatile deserves to get all wrapped up in loveliness.

1. Cut off the top of your cereal box.

2. Reinforce the bottom with the strong packing tape.

3. Use the ruler to measure the remaining panels and jot down these dimensions with the pencil.

4. Pick which sections of gift wrap best fit the different panels. Mark and cut them out. I used one style of paper for the front and back, and a coordinating paper for the sides.

5. Seal these pieces in place with the Mod Podge (read directions on container). Be sure to smooth out any crinkles and bubbles during this process!

6. While the box is drying, snip the ribbon to the desired length and glue each end flat to the inner, side panels of the box to create a strap. For extra strength, reinforce the ribbon with strong packing tape.

7. Measure and cut your felt into a flap for the top of the bag. I cut a free-form curve on one end to give it more flair.

8. If you wish, cut a decorative fabric shape that echos that of your felt flap. Glue it in place on top of the felt.

9. Now glue the back edge of the flap to the inner back panel so that it folds down over the front of your box.

10. While everything is drying, add the two self-stick Velcro dots to where the underside of the flap meets the box. Now your bag can safely keep her secret identity hidden!

Sack These Supplies!

- 1 empty cereal box
- craft scissors
- strong packing tape
- ruler
- pencil
- assorted sheets of gift wrap
- Mod Podge craft adhesive
- 1 long piece of ribbon (same width as box depth)
- craft glue or hot glue gun and glue sticks
- marker
- felt (for the flap)
- decorative fabric (optional—for the flap)
- 2 self-stick Velcro dots

What's in the bag?

The structural nature of Cereal Style makes it nifty for keeping small documents.

Gothic Romance Book Bag

There are some girls who always prefer a dark and stormy night.

1. Spend some time at used bookstores, flea markets, or tag sales to find a sturdy old hardcover book and a paperback novel with a fabulous cover.

2. Carefully remove the pages of the hardcover book by snipping out 7 to 10 pages at a time with sharp scissors.

3. Paint the front and back covers of the hardcover book. Choose a color that will go well with the paperback novel you've selected. Allow about one hour of drying time.

4. Now for a big decision! There are two choices. You can cut the cover off of your paperback book, or you can make a color copy of it so that the book won't be coverless. If you choose the latter, be sure to glue the photocopy to the piece of thick paper for strength, and cut to size.

5. Coat the cover with Mod Podge craft sealer so that it's weatherproof.

6. Glue the paperback cover in place using craft glue. Use the photo corners for extra decoration.

7. Cut the two expanding accordion ends off of a small expanding file folder and trim them to fit the ends of the hardcover book.

8. Hot-glue them in place so that the hardcover book becomes an expanding pocket.

9. If the base corners need little strips of felt to fill in the gaps, now is the time to glue them in place.

10. Fasten the handles to the inside or outside of the pocket (depending on depth) by cutting little felt rectangles, looping them around the attachment points, and hot-gluing them in place. If you're feeling romantic, glue lace trim to the handles for extra flounce.

11. Slip in a spine-chilling novella and be on your blustery way!

Sack These Supplies!

- 1 discarded hardcover book (with at least a one-inch spine)
- 1 slightly smaller Gothic romance paperback book
- craft scissors
- pearlescent or metallic craft paint
- paintbrush
- thick paper (optional—to fit the paperback cover)
- Mod Podge craft sealer
- craft glue
- 4 photo corners
- 1 small expanding file folder
- hot glue gun and glue sticks
- 1 scrap of felt
- 1 set of handbag handles
- lace trim (optional—for handles)

What's in the bag?

Why, your favorite tale of terror, of course!

The Enchanting Evening Bag

The city lights are all a-twinkle as you step onto the pink carpet. Cameras have no choice but to turn your way.

"Who is this captivating scene stealer and how can I bag her dazzling style?"

When the sun goes down, your evening bag's flair only flourishes.

The Natty Necklace Bag

*Elegant necklaces display a certain savoir faire that says,
"Yes! I do know how to paint the town!"*

1. Try arranging your necklaces and brooch in different ways to see which configuration best suits the purse that you have chosen for this project.

2. Once you are happy with your design, sew the necklaces in place. I sewed my necklaces at each end and then let the middle sections drape down over the bag.

3. Pin your brooch in place.

4. Using your best style judgment, decide whether you want to sew on any felt swirls, ribbon, or netting for added style. If attending a Princess Cotillion, your proper purse awaits!

Sack These Supplies!

- 1 abandoned cloth or soft leather purse
- 2–3 inexpensive yet stylish necklaces
- 1 brooch
- strong needle and thread
- craft scissors
- assorted pieces of felt, ribbon, or netting (optional—for embellishment)

Rags to Riches... and Then Some!

Are your silky old PJs looking a little raggedy?
Here's their chance to be reborn!

1. Cut your pajama bottoms into strips that are approximately 2" x 4". Don't worry if the strips are not very even or consistent. Once they're glued in place, their shape won't matter.

2. One by one, glue the center section of the strips to the bag until it is completely covered. It is best to work from one end of the purse to the other to avoid bare patches. Also, you can glue more than one area of the strip down to the purse for extra coverage; just be sure not to pull any of the pieces too taut or else the bag might pucker.

3. Scrunch up the small scrap of velvet and glue it to the top left-hand corner of your bag.

4. Arrange and glue the feathers within the tousled velvet.

5. If your bag is made of mesh material, hook the ends of your necklace through the mesh to make a strap. If the ends don't hook, use the needle and thread to sew them to the pocketbook.

6. Measure, mark, and cut a piece of cardboard that is slightly smaller than your bag. Slip it inside to provide structure and sturdiness.

7. Bravo! Bravo! Give this evening bag a hand!

Sack These Supplies!

- 1 long, medium-size receipt bag (preferably mesh)
- 1 pair silky old pajama bottoms
- craft scissors
- hot glue gun and glue sticks
- a small amount of velvet (a scrap will do)
- 4–5 feathers
- 1 long, fake gold chain with hook-style clasp
- strong needle and thread (if needed)
- 1 long piece of cardboard

What's in the bag?

This one's marvelous for taking home playbills after a night at the theater.

Gem of a Pocketbook

Attention! Attention! Summoning all glamour gals!
Sparkly powers, ACTIVATE.

1. Paint your entire box a bright, gem-toned color and allow about an hour of drying time.

2. Lay your box face-down on the fetching piece of fabric and trace around the edges with the marker.

3. Cut this contour out and glue it to the front of the box.

4. Cut the felt scraps into decorative shapes and combine them with the old jewelry, craft gems, and beads to create a dazzling design.

5. Glue everything in place. If your jewelry is a bit heavy, glue small tabs of felt over the fastening pin, earring clip, or other appropriate hardware to hold it securely.

6. Now for the handle! First gently hammer the nail into the top of your box to create two small holes that correspond to where your handle should go. You may need to twist the nail to remove it.

7. Thread a large bead onto the bead wire and twist the end of the wire around the bead a few times so that it can't slip off. Thread the loose end of the wire up through the hole you have made in the top of the box, leaving the bead on the inside and a length of wire poking up on the outside. (The bead will act as a knot to keep your handle in place.)

8. Thread beads onto the wire until the handle is exactly the length you would like it to be. Now push the wire down through the other hole and into the purse.

9. With the end of the handle, repeat step 7 and clip off any excess wire with the wire clippers. Such shimmery splendor!

Sack These Supplies!

- 1 wooden box with a latch
- pearlescent or metallic craft paint
- paintbrush
- pretty fabric (to cover the box front)
- marker
- craft scissors
- craft glue and hot glue gun and glue sticks
- assorted scraps of felt
- assorted thrift store brooches or broken jewelry
- assorted craft gems
- assorted large, shimmery beads
- 1 small hammer and 1 tiny nail
- strong bead wire (for the handle)
- wire clippers

Design Diva

This purse is inspired by the great handbag designer Enid Collins. She is best known for her themed wooden-box and canvas bucket-style bags, whimsically adorned with paint, faux gems, and other bits of sparkly hardware. Enid did most of her designing in the 1960s, but her work is still collected and prized by connoisseurs of cuteness. Maybe one day your bags will be fought over by collectors, too!

Winged Sophisticate

Spread your wings and show the world how to sparkle!

1. First, lay your pocketbook aside and focus on making a divine dragonfly. On the plain paper, draw a long, narrow wing, either inspired by this photo or by one from a nature magazine. Then draw a slightly smaller wing to match.

2. Cut out these shapes and trace them twice onto the sheer green fabric. Cut them out so you have two big wings and two small wings.

3. If desired, cut curvy decorative shapes out of the turquoise felt and glue them on top of your wings. (You may want to make a paper template for these, too.)

4. Create a dragonfly body by cutting about five long, skinny, semitriangular shapes out of the green felt and gluing them in an overlapping fashion.

5. Now decorate your buggy little friend by gluing the large green button at the head and the medium green buttons down the body.

6. Add the two yellow buttons for eyes and the green heart-shaped gems for glamour.

7. Sparkles take flight! Glitterize the edge of your wings and glue them to the underside of the body.

8. If your shimmery creation needs extra support, cut a long, thin piece of green felt and glue it to the underside as well.

9. Glue the dragonfly onto your blue bag. If you want Ms. Dragonfly to be a removable creature feature instead, simply make her into a pin rather than securing her permanently with glue. To do this, glue a little strip of felt over the stable bar of the safety pin to anchor it onto the back of the dragonfly. (Hold firmly until the glue dries.)

10. With this purse on your arm, the buzz on the street will be that you never let your dazzle frazzle!

Sack These Supplies!

- 1 blue pocketbook of any size or shape
- plain paper for making a pattern
- green marker
- craft scissors
- sheer green fabric (for the dragonfly wings)
- 1 scrap of turquoise felt (optional)
- craft glue
- green felt (for the dragonfly body)
- 1 large and 3 medium-size green buttons
- 2 yellow buttons
- 4 green heart-shaped gems
- iridescent green glitter or glitter glue
- safety pin (optional)

What's in the bag?

Sheer, sparkling face powder (you don't want your dragonfly to be the only one twinkling about)!

Golden Delirium Disco Sash

If you have over-the-top panache, this belted disco bag might be exactly what you're looking for!

1. Trim the marabou to your desired length by wrapping it around your waist so that the two ends dangle down to about mid-thigh. Cut off the excess.

2. Sew the top middle edge of one of the gift bags to one of the ends of the marabou.

3. Repeat this step with your remaining bag and the opposite end of the marabou.

4. Sew or glue one decorative butterfly onto each bag.

5. Wear with flair—you are now the golden goddess of the dance floor!

Sack These Supplies!

- 1 long piece of thin marabou
- craft scissors
- needle and thread
- 2 sheer gold fabric gift bags with drawstrings
- 2 decorative craft butterflies
- craft glue (optional)

What's in the bag?

Since you'll be groovin' all night, you'll need your hands free. This bag is perfect for stowing lightweight gear like your house key, a few dollars, and lip gloss.

The Allure of Accessories

*O*ftentimes, all a weary old bag needs is a little extra attention to detail in order to make a stunning transformation. That's where alluring accessories make their grand appearance. Brooches, keychains, pom-poms, and ID tags are all cinchy ways to go from plain Jane to voguish urbane in a matter of minutes!

Keychains to Dazzle

Keychains are a charming way to add twinkling finesse to many a bag. Simply sew any spectacular little doodad or frill frippery that strikes your fancy to a ready–made key loop or chain, and you're ready to go!

Some Ideas for Stuff to Dangle

* tiny toys from a gumball machine

* earrings that have lost their mates

* initial or monogram patches

* one-of-a-kind beads
  (the bigger, the better!)

* fabric flowers

* laminated stickers or photos

* holiday craft novelties (bitty bunnies,
  tiny trees . . . you get the picture)

* playing cards

* pom-poms

* tassels

* decorated felt or crafting foam shapes

Sack These Supplies!

* key loop and chain
  (sold in craft stores)

* if it dangles, chain it . . .
  the sky is the limit!

* strong needle and thread

* craft scissors

Brooches and Pins-a-Plenty!

I can't sing the praises of pins and brooches enough. They quickly cover up unsightly stains on old but beautiful bags. They add asymmetrical grace when pinned in just the right place. And they can be changed often to go with the theme of the outfit you are wearing for that day or evening. Does multifaceted flair get any better?

Brooch It!

Look around your closet or craft bins for eye-catching decorative details, such as:

* feathers (peacock feathers make gorgeous brooches)
* craft store butterflies and birds
* oversized bows and ribbon bursts
* small sections of decorative fabric
* felt shapes made from the templates in this book
* trinkets 'n treasures of old
* discarded jewelry
* fabric leaves
* fabric flowers
* pom-poms
* painted shells
* a combination of these!

Making a Pin. . .

Take a good gander at what you wish to convert into a brooch and ponder the possibilities for securing it to the clasp. Feather stems can be wrapped in ribbon and adhered to the pin. Craft store butterflies, birds, flowers, and leaves can be sewn or glued directly to the clasp. One of my favorite ways to make a pin is to enlarge or reduce the templates in this book and transfer them onto felt. Depending on fragility, I also glue that shape onto cardboard for strength. Then I decorate the felt with patterned fabric, sparkles, beads, and other such crafty garnish.

I often use large safety pins as clasps because they are so strong and very inexpensive. Just glue a little strip of felt over the stable bar of the safety pin to anchor it onto the backing material. (Hold firmly until the glue dries.)

Sack These Supplies!

* assorted objects you wish to transform into brooches
* large safety pins or clasp bases
* craft glue or hot glue gun and glue sticks
* felt
* cardboard (needed to reinforce heavier objects)

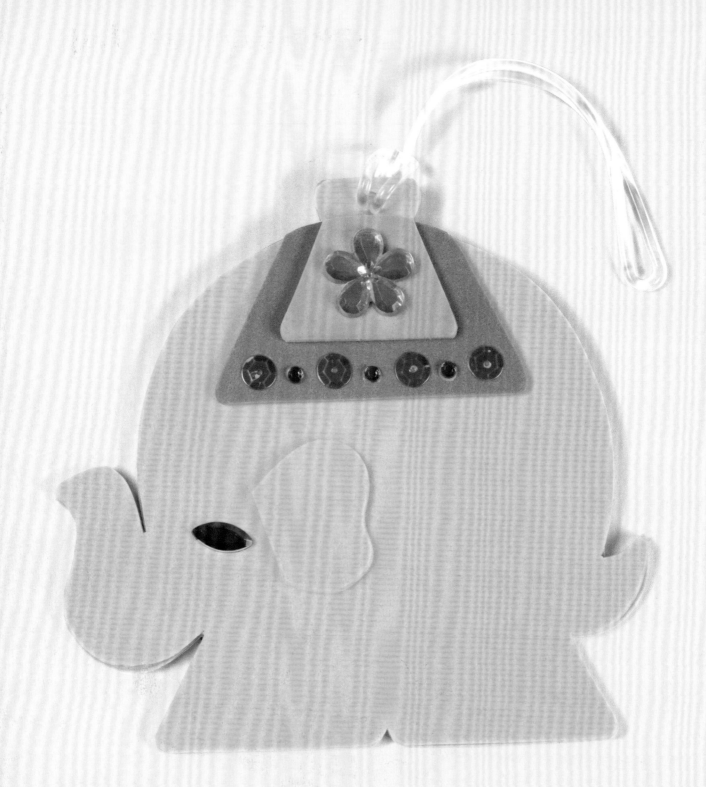

Pinky the Pachyderm Luggage Tag

She's quite a globe trotter, that elephant gal!

1. Use the elephant template from page 109 to trace and cut two pachyderm contours out of the pink crafting foam. (Be sure to flip the pattern in the process so you'll have two shapes that fit together back to back, sandwiching your marker lines inside.) Save the scraps.

2. Punch a little hole in the tab at the top of each elephant shape.

3. Choose a circle stencil that is about 2 1/2 inches in diameter. Trace it onto the back of your luggage tag and cut it out.

4. Cut a slightly larger circle out of the clear vinyl to fit *behind* the circular hole you've cut. Glue it in place to make a window.

5. Glue the elephant pieces together at the edges (marker lines facing inward), leaving an opening at the top and space in the middle for your ID info.

6. Use the elephant carpet template from page 109 to trace the carpet shapes onto the brown and tan crafting foam. Cut them out and glue them to the front of your elephant.

7. Now trace a cute little ear on a scrap of pink foam, cut it out, and glue it to the front as well.

8. Decorate your pachyderm with gems and sequins, saving a special gem just for her eye. Be sure to allow at least an hour of drying time.

9. On the small piece of heavy paper (sized to fit the window at the back), write your ID info and slip it into place.

10. Attach the length of luggage cord or ribbon through the hole you've punched in the elephant's top tabs.

11. Take Pinky the Pachyderm along on a very exciting adventure!

Sack These Supplies!

- elephant template from page 109
- dark pink marker
- craft scissors
- 1 sheet pink crafting foam
- hole punch
- circle stencils (from art or craft store)
- clear vinyl (for tag window)
- craft glue
- 1 small scrap of brown crafting foam
- 1 small scrap of tan crafting foam
- an assortment of faux gems and sequins
- 1 small piece of heavy paper
- fine-point permanent marker
- 1 length of plastic luggage cord or strong narrow ribbon

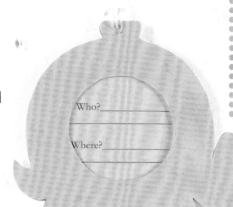

Who?_____
_____
Where?_____
_____

Where to Put Those Pom-Poms!

Pom-poms have so much personality that it's hard to refrain from sticking them everywhere! Here are a few of my favorite ways to put those fuzzy-wuzzies to work:

* Sew them onto zipper pulls

* Attach them to keychains

* Glue a gigantic pom-pom on to a compact lid

* String a bunch together to make a handle

* Turn an extra-special pom-pom into a pin

* Sew on some fringey snippets of yarn and it's a tassel!

* Make a special pom-pom bag, covered completely in you-know-whats!

Pom-Poms Are Forever!

The quirky softness and style of pom–poms is timeless.

1. To create a pom-pom maker, use one of the circle stencils to trace two $2^1/_2$ inch circles onto the cardboard. Cut out both circles. Cut a hole in the center of each circle and then widen the hole carefully with the scissors until it is about $7/_8$ of an inch wide. (You can use your circle stencil as a guide in making this hole instead.) Cut a slit leading from the outer edge to the hole in the middle. The shape you have created should look like a fat letter "C" (or a donut with a very skinny little slice cut through one side).

2. Place the two pieces together, like two halves of a sandwich, with the slits lined up. You now have a pom-pom maker!

3. Starting near the slit, wrap yarnaround the arm of the pom-pom maker. Be sure to overlap the yarn evenly. Keep wrapping until you get around to the other end of the "C."

4. Then start wrapping in the other direction.

5. Keep wrapping, around and around the "C" shape until the middle section of the pom-pom maker is all filled up, and it's difficult to keep going. Snip the end of your yarn.

6. Then, starting at the slit, nudge the blade of your scissors in between the two cardboard pieces.

7. Carefully cut the yarn, snipping all the way around until you reach the other end.

8. Do not remove your pom-pom maker yet!!!

9. Cut a 7- or 8-inch piece of yarn and tie it tightly around the yarn you have just cut, in between the two pieces of cardboard.

10. You may want to pull the yarn twice around. When everything feels tight, tie the yarn in a very strong knot. Cut the ends and remove the cardboard.

11. Fluff out the pom-pom to see how cute it looks!

12. Trim any stray tufts or wayward yarn bits. Depending on the type of yarn used, your pom-pom may need just a little snip or a major haircut.

13. Experiment with sizes by enlarging the pom-pom maker on a copy machine. It's also fun to try using different types of yarn. There are so many colors and textures to choose from that the results are truly bonkers!

Sack These Supplies!

- circle stencils (from art or craft store)
- marker or pencil
- sturdy cardboard
- craft scissors
- circle stencils (optional)
- ruler
- yarn

Templates

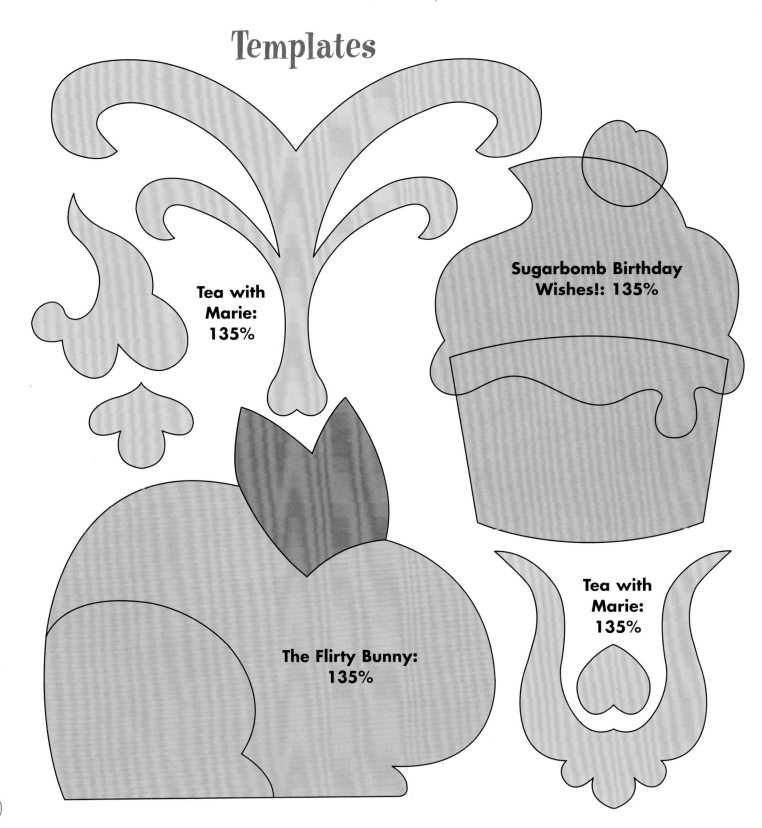

Tea with Marie: 135%

Sugarbomb Birthday Wishes!: 135%

The Flirty Bunny: 135%

Tea with Marie: 135%

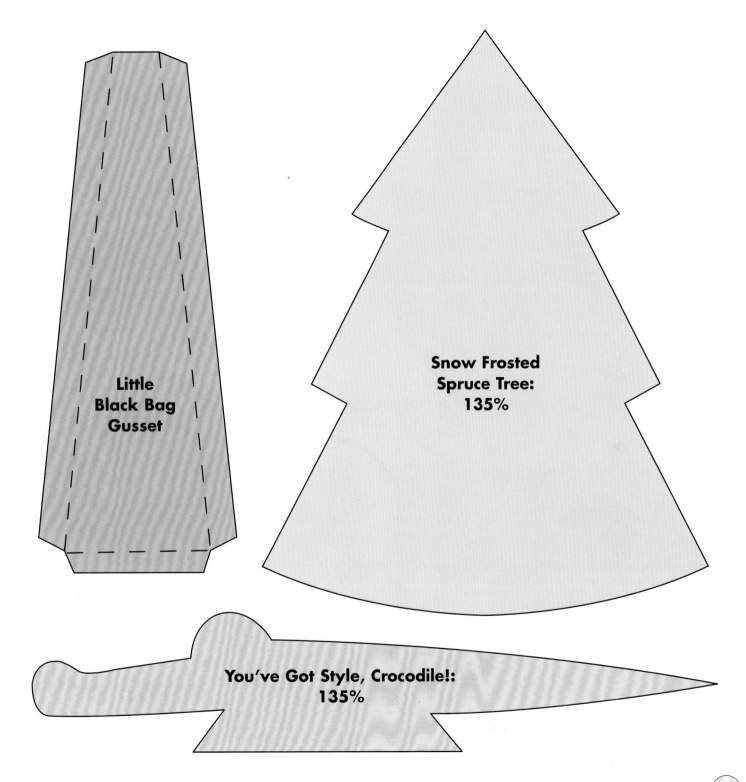

Little
Black Bag
Gusset

Snow Frosted
Spruce Tree:
135%

You've Got Style, Crocodile!:
135%

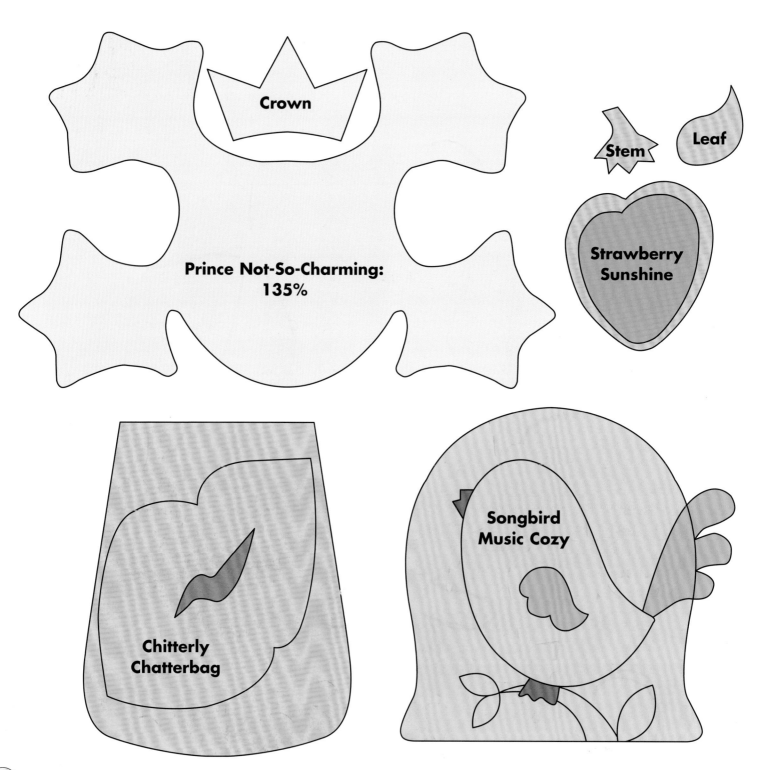

Crown

Stem

Leaf

Prince Not-So-Charming:
135%

Strawberry
Sunshine

Chitterly
Chatterbag

Songbird
Music Cozy

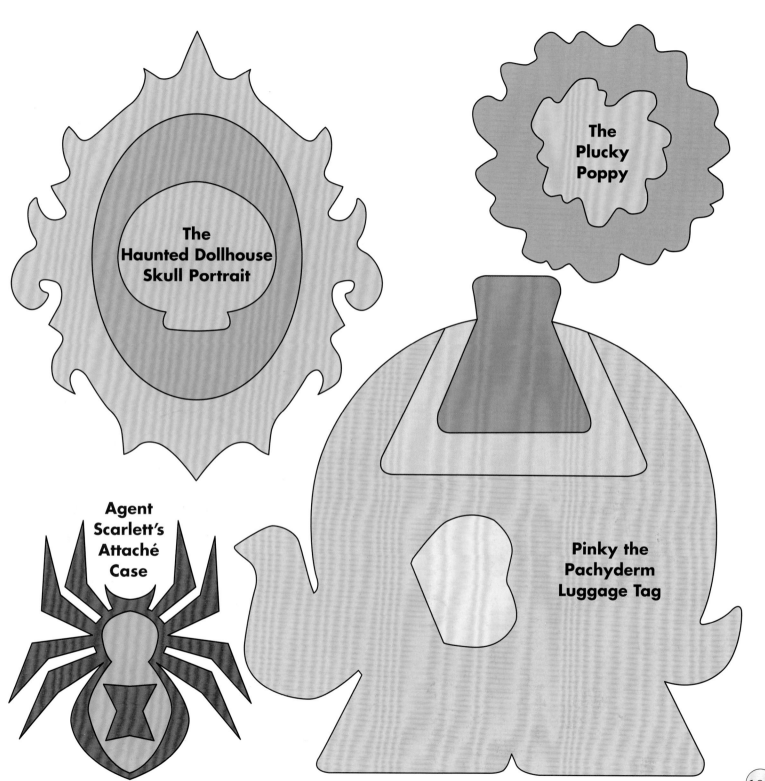

The
Haunted Dollhouse
Skull Portrait

The
Plucky
Poppy

Agent
Scarlett's
Attaché
Case

Pinky the
Pachyderm
Luggage Tag

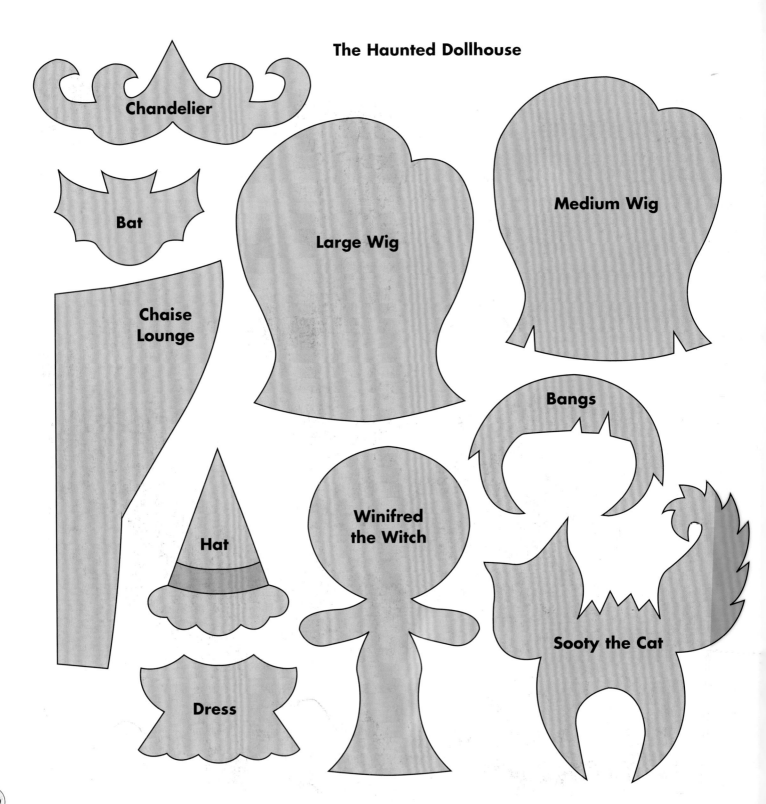

The Haunted Dollhouse

Chandelier

Bat

Large Wig

Medium Wig

Chaise Lounge

Bangs

Hat

Winifred the Witch

Dress

Sooty the Cat

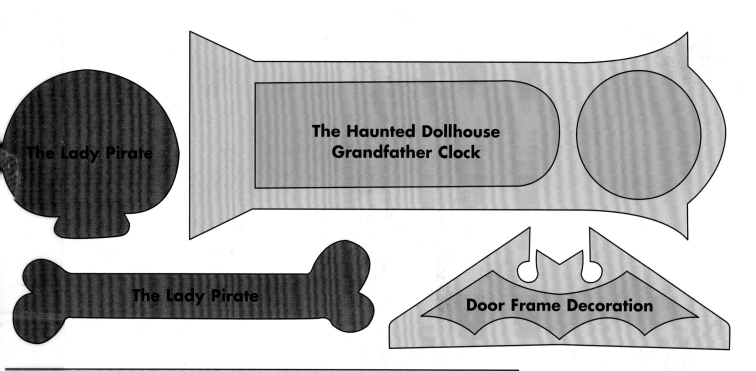

The Lady Pirate

The Haunted Dollhouse
Grandfather Clock

The Lady Pirate

Door Frame Decoration

The Haunted Dollhouse Fireplace

The Haunted
Dollhouse
Door

Index

Metric Conversion Chart

Imperial (Inches)	Metric (Centimeters)
⅛	0.3
¼	0.6
½	1.3
¾	1.9
1	2.5
1¼	3.2
1½	3.8
1¾	4.4
2	5.1
2½	6.4
3	7.6
3½	8.9
4	10.2
4½	11.4
5	12.7
5½	14.0
6	15.2
6½	16.5
7	17.8
7½	19.0
8	20.3
8½	21.6
9	22.9
9½	24.1
10	25.4
11	27.9
12	30.5
13	33.0
14	35.6
15	38.1
16	40.6
17	43.2
18	45.7
19	48.3
20	50.8
25	63.5
30	76.2
35	88.9
40	101.6